To

From

Hidden in My Heart

Daily Scripture from the King James Version.

Published by Garborg's®, a brand of DaySpring® Cards, Inc.
Siloam Springs, Arkansas

Scripture quotations are taken from the King James Version of the Bible.

ISBN 1-58061-745-X

JANUARY 1

And we know that all things work together for good to them that love God, to them who are the called according to his purpose.

ROMANS 8:28

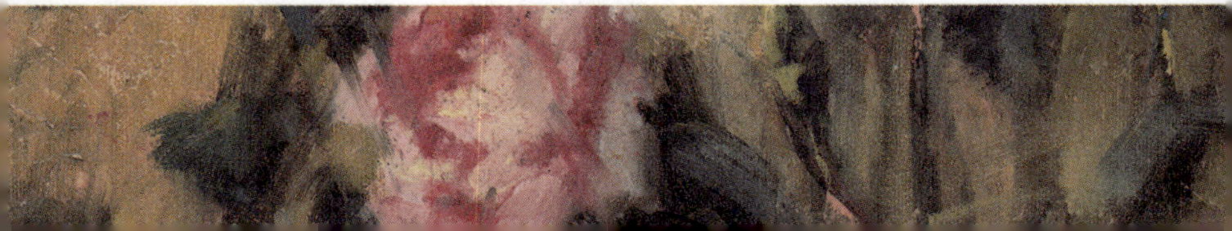

DECEMBER 31

*G*race unto you, and peace, from God our Father and the Lord Jesus Christ.

2 THESSALONIANS 1:2

JANUARY 2

Peace I leave with you, my peace I give unto you: not as the world giveth, give I unto you. Let not your heart be troubled, neither let it be afraid.

JOHN 14:27

DECEMBER 30

So shall the knowledge of wisdom be unto thy soul: when thou hast found it, then there shall be a reward, and thy expectation shall not be cut off.

PROVERBS 24:14

JANUARY 3

Then spake Jesus again unto them, saying, I am the light of the world: he that followeth me shall not walk in darkness, but shall have the light of life.

JOHN 8:12

DECEMBER 29

But the God of all grace, who hath called us unto his eternal glory by Christ Jesus, after that ye have suffered a while, make you perfect, stablish, strengthen, settle you.

1 Peter 5:10

JANUARY 4

They that wait upon the Lord shall renew their strength; they shall mount up with wings as eagles; they shall run, and not be weary; and they shall walk, and not faint.

ISAIAH 40:31

DECEMBER 28

Servants, be obedient to them that are your masters,...With good will doing service, as to the Lord, and not to men: Knowing that whatsoever good thing any man doeth, the same shall he receive of the Lord, whether he be bond or free.

EPHESIANS 6:5,7-8

JANUARY 5

Wait on the Lord: be of good courage,
and he shall strengthen thine heart:
wait, I say, on the Lord.

PSALM 27:14

DECEMBER 27

Arise, shine; for thy light is come, and the glory of the Lord is risen upon thee. For, behold, the darkness shall cover the earth, and gross darkness the people: but the Lord shall arise upon thee, and his glory shall be seen upon thee.

ISAIAH 60:1–2

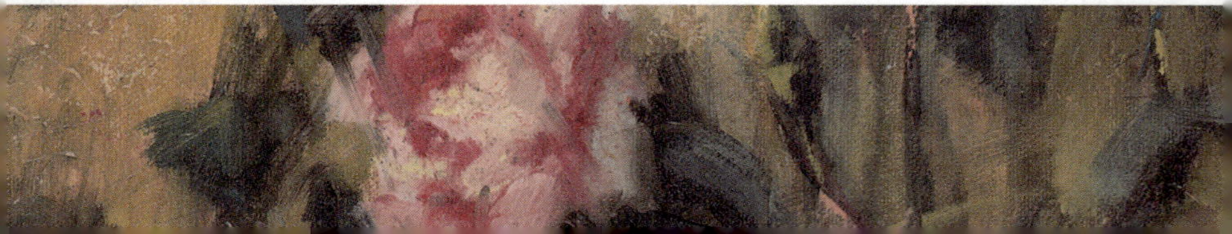

JANUARY 6

Come unto me, all ye that labour and are heavy laden, and I will give you rest. Take my yoke upon you, and learn of me; for I am meek and lowly in heart: and ye shall find rest unto your souls.

MATTHEW 11:28–29

DECEMBER 26

Thanks be unto God for
his unspeakable gift.

2 Corinthians 9:15

JANUARY 7

Delight thyself also in the Lord; and he shall give thee the desires of thine heart. Commit thy way unto the Lord; trust also in him; and he shall bring it to pass. And he shall bring forth thy righteousness as the light, and thy judgment as the noonday.

PSALM 37:4–6

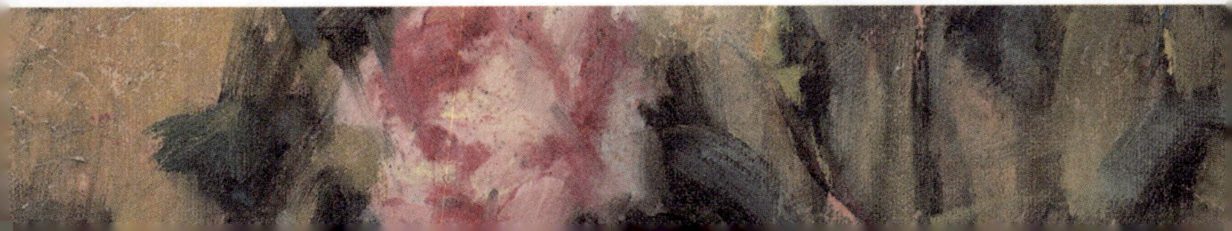

DECEMBER 25

For unto us a child is born, unto us a son is given: and the government shall be upon his shoulder: and his name shall be called Wonderful, Counsellor, The mighty God, The everlasting Father, The Prince of Peace.

ISAIAH 9:6

JANUARY 8

Study to shew thyself approved unto God, a workman that needeth not to be ashamed, rightly dividing the word of truth.

2 TIMOTHY 2:15

DECEMBER 24

Behold, a virgin shall be with child, and shall bring forth a son, and they shall call his name Emmanuel, which being interpreted is, God with us.

MATTHEW 1:23

JANUARY 9

Be still, and know that I am God...
I will be exalted in the earth. The Lord of hosts
is with us; the God of Jacob is our refuge.

PSALM 46:10–11

DECEMBER 23

And of his fulness have all we received, and grace for grace. For the law was given by Moses, but grace and truth came by Jesus Christ.

JOHN 1:16–17

JANUARY 10

They that trust in the Lord shall be as mount Zion, which cannot be removed, but abideth for ever. As the mountains are round about Jerusalem, so the Lord is round about his people from henceforth even for ever.

PSALM 125:1–2

DECEMBER 22

It is more blessed to give than to receive.

Acts 20:35

JANUARY 11

Rest in the Lord, and wait patiently for him: fret not thyself because of him who prospereth in his way, because of the man who bringeth wicked devices to pass. Cease from anger, and forsake wrath: fret not thyself in any wise to do evil.

PSALM 37:7–8

DECEMBER 21

Give, and it shall be given unto you; good measure, pressed down, and shaken together, and running over, shall men give into your bosom. For with the same measure that ye mete withal it shall be measured to you again.

LUKE 6:38

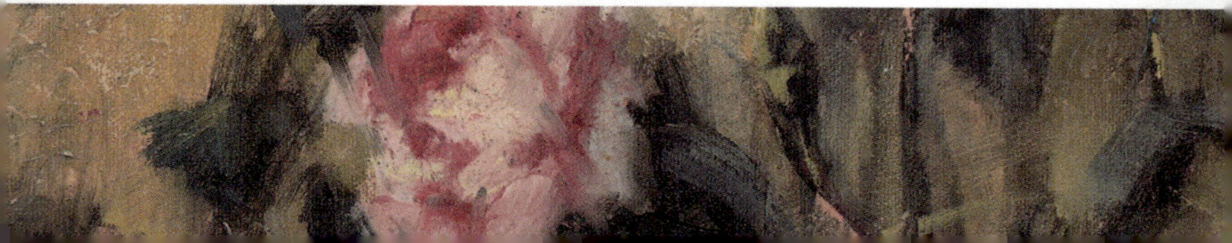

JANUARY 12

I am the door: by me if any man enter in, he shall be saved, and shall go in and out, and find pasture. The thief cometh not, but for to steal, and to kill, and to destroy: I am come that they might have life, and that they might have it more abundantly. I am the good shepherd: the good shepherd giveth his life for the sheep.

JOHN 10:9–11

DECEMBER 20

And she shall bring forth a son, and thou shalt call his name Jesus: for he shall save his people from their sins.

MATTHEW 1:21

JANUARY 13

He calleth his own sheep by name, and leadeth them out. And when he putteth forth his own sheep, he goeth before them, and the sheep follow him: for they know his voice.

JOHN 10:3–4

DECEMBER 19

For thou, Lord, hast made me glad through thy work: I will triumph in the works of thy hands. O Lord, how great are thy works! and thy thoughts are very deep.

PSALM 92:4–5

JANUARY 14

Pray without ceasing. In every thing give thanks: for this is the will of God in Christ Jesus concerning you.

1 THESSALONIANS 5:17–18

DECEMBER 18

And the Word was made flesh, and dwelt among us, (and we beheld his glory, the glory as of the only begotten of the Father,) full of grace and truth.

JOHN 1:14

JANUARY 15

Jesus came and spake unto them, saying, All power is given unto me in heaven and in earth. Go ye therefore, and teach all nations, baptizing them in the name of the Father, and of the Son, and of the Holy Ghost.

MATTHEW 28:18–19

DECEMBER 17

Thy kingdom come. Thy will be done in earth, as it is in heaven.

MATTHEW 6:10

JANUARY 16

Then came the word of the Lord unto Jeremiah, saying, Behold, I am the Lord, the God of all flesh: is there any thing too hard for me?

JEREMIAH 32:26–27

DECEMBER 16

The rich and poor meet together: the Lord is the maker of them all.

PROVERBS 22:2

JANUARY 17

Trust in the Lord with all thine heart; and lean not unto thine own understanding. In all thy ways acknowledge him, and he shall direct thy paths.

PROVERBS 3:5-6

DECEMBER 15

Cast thy bread upon the waters:
for thou shalt find it after many days.

ECCLESIASTES 11:1

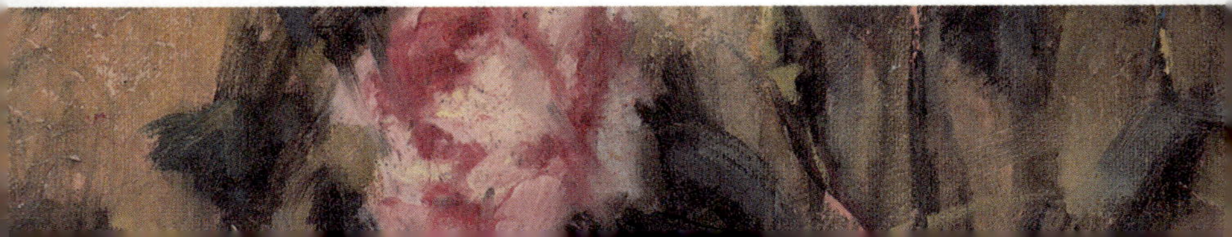

JANUARY 18

Now unto him that is able to do exceeding abundantly above all that we ask or think, according to the power that worketh in us.

EPHESIANS 3:20

DECEMBER 14

There is one God; and there is none other but he: And to love him with all the heart, and with all the understanding, and with all the soul, and with all the strength, and to love his neighbour as himself, is more than all whole burnt offerings and sacrifices.

MARK 12:32-33

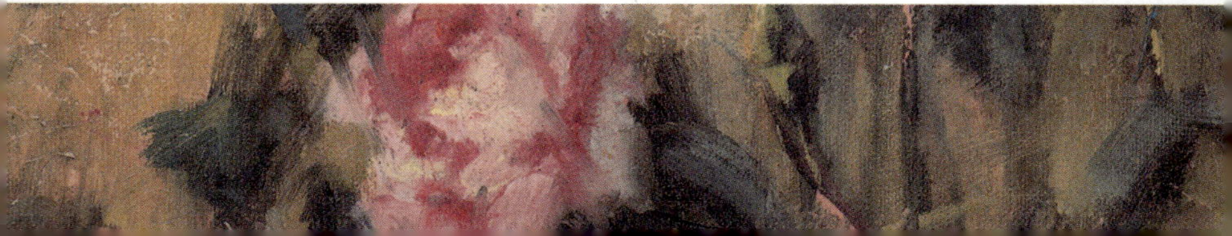

JANUARY 19

For this cause I bow my knees unto the Father of our Lord Jesus Christ...That Christ may dwell in your hearts by faith; that ye, being rooted and grounded in love, May be able to comprehend with all saints what is the breadth, and length, and depth, and height; And to know the love of Christ, which passeth knowledge, that ye might be filled with all the fulness of God.

EPHESIANS 3:14,16–19

DECEMBER 13

Who remembered us in our low estate: for his mercy endureth for ever.

PSALM 136:23

JANUARY 20

For as he thinketh in his heart, so is he.

PROVERBS 23:7

DECEMBER 12

And thou, child, shalt be called the prophet of the Highest:... Through the tender mercy of our God; whereby the dayspring from on high hath visited us, To give light to them that sit in darkness and in the shadow of death, to guide our feet into the way of peace.

LUKE 1:76–79

JANUARY 21

Be content with such things as ye have: for he hath said, I will never leave thee, nor forsake thee.

HEBREWS 13:5

DECEMBER 11

Jesus answered and said unto him, If a man love me, he will keep my words: and my Father will love him, and we will come unto him, and make our abode with him.

JOHN 14:23

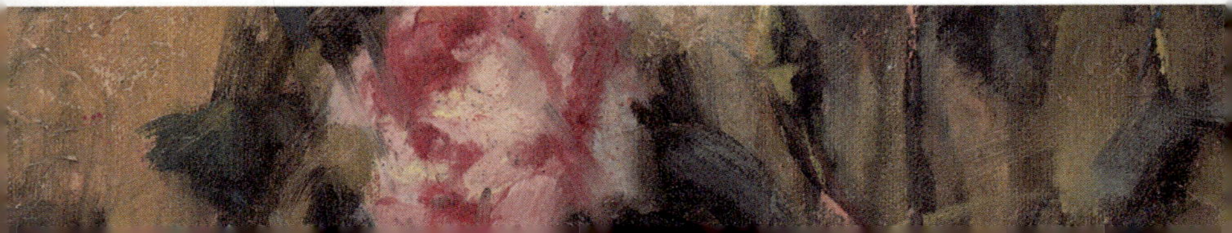

JANUARY 22

Fear thou not; for I am with thee: be not dismayed; for I am thy God: I will strengthen thee; yea, I will help thee; yea, I will uphold thee with the right hand of my righteousness.

ISAIAH 41:10

DECEMBER 10

Ye are a chosen generation, a royal priesthood,
an holy nation, a peculiar people; that ye
should shew forth the praises of him who hath
called you out of darkness into his marvellous light.

1 PETER 2:9

JANUARY 23

He that dwelleth in the secret place of the most High shall abide under the shadow of the Almighty. I will say of the Lord, He is my refuge and my fortress: my God; in him will I trust.

PSALM 91:1-2

DECEMBER 9

I cried unto the Lord with my voice; with my voice unto the Lord did I make my supplication.... When my spirit was overwhelmed within me, then thou knewest my path. In the way wherein I walked have they privily laid a snare for me.

PSALM 142:1,3

JANUARY 24

I am the vine, ye are the branches: He that abideth in me, and I in him, the same bringeth forth much fruit: for without me ye can do nothing.

John 15:5

DECEMBER 8

For the bread of God is he which cometh down from heaven, and giveth life unto the world.

John 6:33

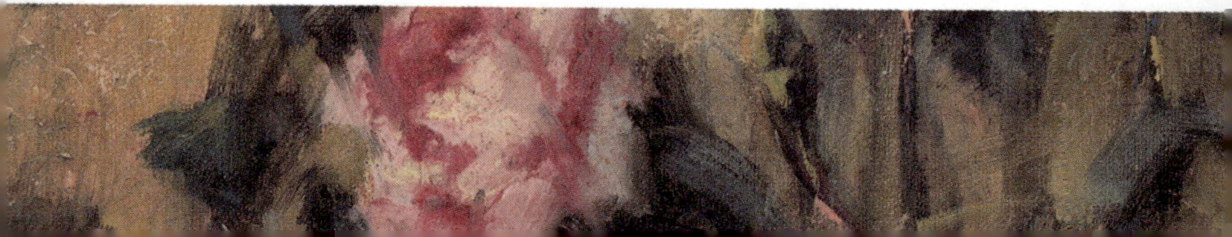

JANUARY 25

We all, with open face beholding as in a glass the glory of the Lord, are changed into the same image from glory to glory, even as by the Spirit of the Lord.

2 Corinthians 3:18

DECEMBER 7

Blessed are the merciful: for they shall obtain mercy. Blessed are the pure in heart: for they shall see God.

MATTHEW 5:7–8

JANUARY 26

Draw nigh to God, and he will draw nigh to you.

JAMES 4:8

DECEMBER 6

But thou, O Lord, art a God full of compassion, and gracious, longsuffering, and plenteous in mercy and truth.

PSALM 86:15

JANUARY 27

Seek ye the kingdom of God; and all these things shall be added unto you.

LUKE 12:31

DECEMBER 5

Be careful for nothing; but in every thing by prayer and supplication with thanksgiving let your requests be made known unto God.

PHILIPPIANS 4:6

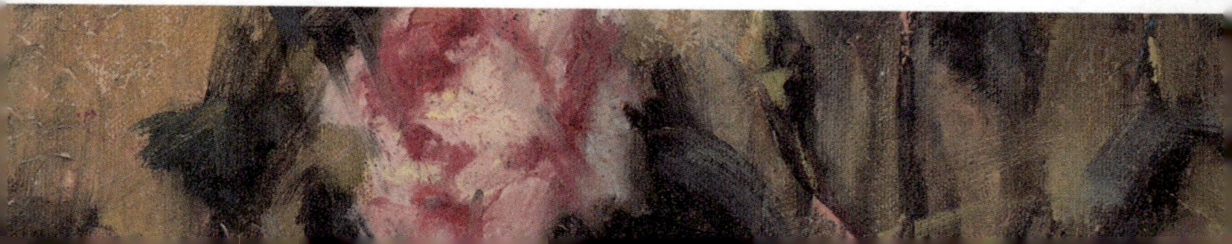

JANUARY 28

I have set the Lord always before me: because he is at my right hand, I shall not be moved.

PSALM 16:8

DECEMBER 4

Let thy mercy, O Lord, be upon us,
according as we hope in thee.

Psalm 33:22

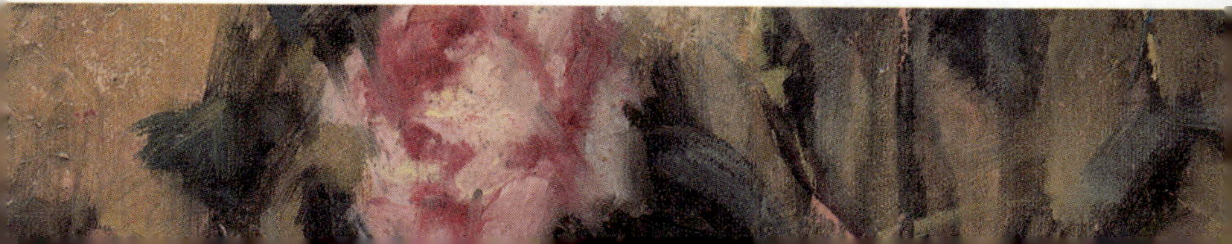

JANUARY 29

Ye have not chosen me, but I have chosen you, and ordained you, that ye should go and bring forth fruit, and that your fruit should remain: that whatsoever ye shall ask of the Father in my name, he may give it you.

JOHN 15:16

DECEMBER 3

The Lord is gracious, and full of compassion; slow to anger, and of great mercy. The Lord is good to all: and his tender mercies are over all his works.

PSALM 145:8–9

JANUARY 30

I beseech you therefore, brethren, by the mercies of God, that ye present your bodies a living sacrifice, holy, acceptable unto God, which is your reasonable service.

ROMANS 12:1

DECEMBER 2

And he said unto his disciples, Therefore I say unto you, Take no thought for your life, what ye shall eat; neither for the body, what ye shall put on. The life is more than meat, and the body is more than raiment.

LUKE 12:22-23

JANUARY 31

Keep thy heart with all diligence;
for out of it are the issues of life.

PROVERBS 4:23

DECEMBER 1

The Lord is slow to anger, and great in power...the Lord hath his way in the whirlwind and in the storm, and the clouds are the dust of his feet.

NAHUM 1:3

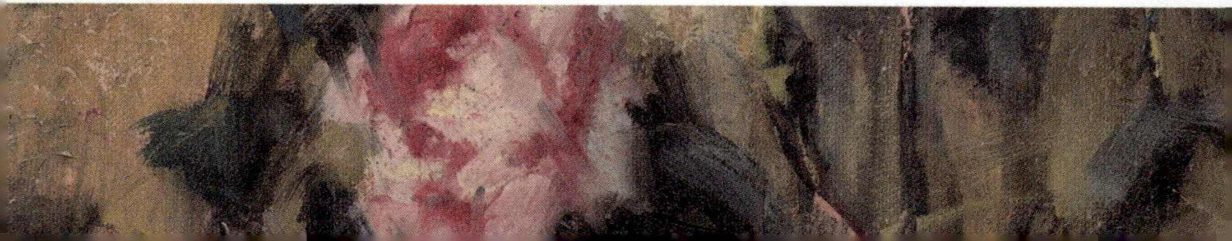

FEBRUARY 1

The joy of the Lord is your strength.

NEHEMIAH 8:10

NOVEMBER 30

Be ye therefore perfect, even as your Father which is in heaven is perfect.

MATTHEW 5:48

FEBRUARY 2

Therefore will the Lord wait, that he may be gracious unto you, and therefore will he be exalted, that he may have mercy upon you: for the Lord is a God of judgment: blessed are all they that wait for him.... He will be very gracious unto thee at the voice of thy cry; when he shall hear it, he will answer thee.

ISAIAH 30:18–19

NOVEMBER 29

I love the Lord, because he hath heard my voice and my supplications. Because he hath inclined his ear unto me, therefore will I call upon him as long as I live.

PSALM 116:1–2

FEBRUARY 3

The steps of a good man are ordered by the Lord: and he delighteth in his way. Though he fall, he shall not be utterly cast down: for the Lord upholdeth him with his hand.

Psalm 37:23–24

NOVEMBER 28

Deep calleth unto deep at the noise of thy waterspouts: all thy waves and thy billows are gone over me.

PSALM 42:7

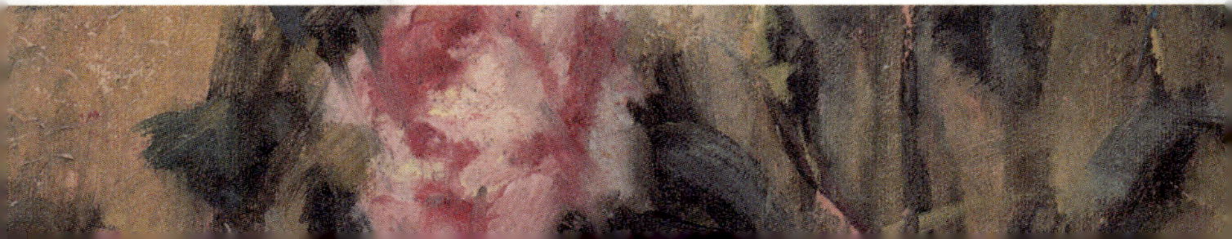

FEBRUARY 4

There hath no temptation taken you but such as is common to man: but God is faithful, who will not suffer you to be tempted above that ye are able; but will with the temptation also make a way to escape, that ye may be able to bear it.

1 Corinthians 10:13

NOVEMBER 27

The day is thine, the night also is thine:
thou hast prepared the light and the sun.
Thou hast set all the borders of the earth:
thou hast made summer and winter.

PSALM 74:16–17

FEBRUARY 5

For I know the thoughts that I think toward you, saith the Lord, thoughts of peace, and not of evil, to give you an expected end.

JEREMIAH 29:11

NOVEMBER 26

God be merciful unto us, and bless us; and cause his face to shine upon us. That thy way may be known upon earth, thy saving health among all nations.

PSALM 67:1-2

FEBRUARY 6

This one thing I do, forgetting those things which are behind, and reaching forth unto those things which are before, I press toward the mark for the prize of the high calling of God in Christ Jesus.

PHILIPPIANS 3:13–14

NOVEMBER 25

But he that is greatest among you shall be your servant. And whosoever shall exalt himself shall be abased; and he that shall humble himself shall be exalted.

MATTHEW 23:11–12

FEBRUARY 7

And whatsoever we ask, we receive of him, because we keep his commandments, and do those things that are pleasing in his sight. And this is his commandment, That we should believe on the name of his Son Jesus Christ, and love one another, as he gave us commandment.

1 JOHN 3:22–23

NOVEMBER 24

O give thanks unto the Lord; for he is good: for his mercy endureth for ever. O give thanks unto the God of gods: for his mercy endureth for ever. O give thanks to the Lord of lords: for his mercy endureth for ever. To him who alone doeth great wonders: for his mercy endureth for ever.

PSALM 136:1–4

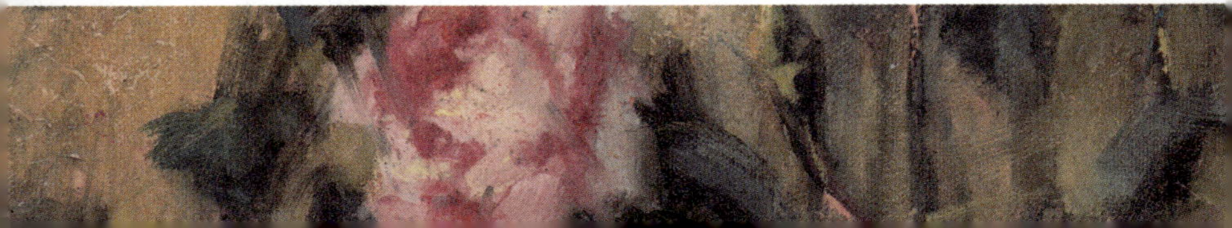

FEBRUARY 8

Be not afraid, only believe.

MARK 5:36

NOVEMBER 23

We give thanks to God always for you all,
making mention of you in our prayers.

1 THESSALONIANS 1:2

FEBRUARY 9

God hath spoken once; twice have I heard this; that power belongeth unto God. Also unto thee, O Lord, belongeth mercy: for thou renderest to every man according to his work.

PSALM 62:11-12

NOVEMBER 22

And the peace of God, which passeth all understanding, shall keep your hearts and minds through Christ Jesus.

PHILIPPIANS 4:7

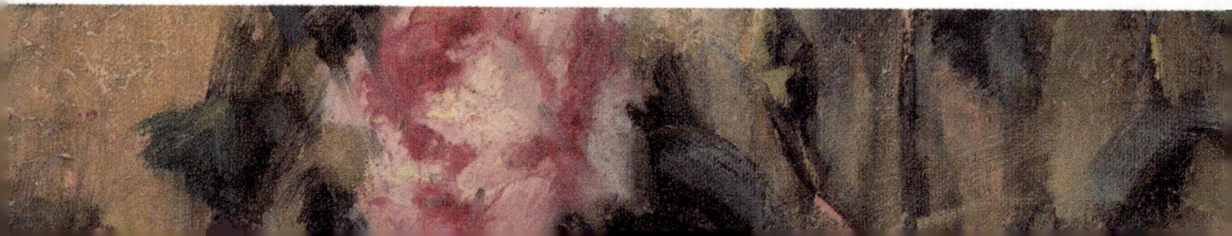

FEBRUARY 10

There is forgiveness with thee, that thou mayest be feared. I wait for the Lord, my soul doth wait, and in his word do I hope. My soul waiteth for the Lord more than they that watch for the morning: I say, more than they that watch for the morning.

PSALM 130:4–6

NOVEMBER 21

Consider the lilies of the field, how they grow; they toil not, neither do they spin: And yet I say unto you, That even Solomon in all his glory was not arrayed like one of these. Wherefore, if God so clothe the grass of the field, which to day is, and to morrow is cast into the oven, shall he not much more clothe you, O ye of little faith?

MATTHEW 6:28–30

FEBRUARY 11

I heard the voice of the Lord, saying,
Whom shall I send, and who will go for us?
Then said I, Here am I; send me.

ISAIAH 6:8

NOVEMBER 20

Therefore it is of faith, that it might be by grace; to the end the promise might be sure to all the seed; not to that only which is of the law, but to that also which is of the faith of Abraham; who is the father of us all.

ROMANS 4:16

FEBRUARY 12

Therefore we are buried with him by baptism into death: that like as Christ was raised up from the dead by the glory of the Father, even so we also should walk in newness of life. For if we have been planted together in the likeness of his death, we shall be also in the likeness of his resurrection.

ROMANS 6:4-5

NOVEMBER 19

Have faith in God. For verily I say unto you, That whosoever shall say unto this mountain, Be thou removed, and be thou cast into the sea; and shall not doubt in his heart, but shall believe that those things which he saith shall come to pass; he shall have whatsoever he saith.

MARK 11:22–23

FEBRUARY 13

Therefore I say unto you, Take no thought for your life, what ye shall eat, or what ye shall drink; nor yet for your body, what ye shall put on. Is not the life more than meat, and the body than raiment? Behold the fowls of the air: for they sow not, neither do they reap, nor gather into barns; yet your heavenly Father feedeth them. Are ye not much better than they?

MATTHEW 6:25-26

NOVEMBER 18

O satisfy us early with thy mercy; that we may rejoice and be glad all our days.

PSALM 90:14

FEBRUARY 14

Hear my cry, O God; attend unto my prayer. From the end of the earth will I cry unto thee, when my heart is overwhelmed: lead me to the rock that is higher than I. For thou hast been a shelter for me, and a strong tower from the enemy.

PSALM 61:1–3

NOVEMBER 17

Canst thou by searching find out God? canst thou find out the Almighty unto perfection? It is as high as heaven; what canst thou do? deeper than hell; what canst thou know? The measure thereof is longer than the earth, and broader than the sea.

JOB 11:7–9

FEBRUARY 15

Wait on the Lord, and keep his way, and he shall exalt thee to inherit the land.

PSALM 37:34

NOVEMBER 16

Wherefore we receiving a kingdom which cannot be moved, let us have grace, whereby we may serve God acceptably with reverence and godly fear.

HEBREWS 12:28

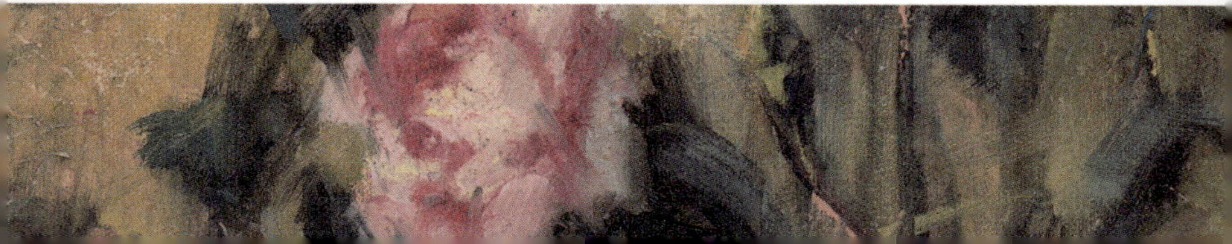

FEBRUARY 16

For as many as are led by the Spirit of God, they are the sons of God. For ye have not received the spirit of bondage again to fear; but ye have received the Spirit of adoption, whereby we cry, Abba, Father.

ROMANS 8:14–15

NOVEMBER 15

The Spirit of God hath made me, and the breath of the Almighty hath given me life.

Job 33:4

FEBRUARY 17

Let us not be weary in well doing: for in due season we shall reap, if we faint not. As we have therefore opportunity, let us do good unto all men, especially unto them who are of the household of faith.

GALATIANS 6:9–10

NOVEMBER 14

Because that which may be known of God is manifest in them; for God hath shewed it unto them. For the invisible things of him from the creation of the world are clearly seen, being understood by the things that are made, even his eternal power and Godhead.

ROMANS 1:19–20

FEBRUARY 18

Whoso findeth me findeth life, and shall obtain favour of the Lord.

PROVERBS 8:35

NOVEMBER 13

For I have satiated the weary soul, and
I have replenished every sorrowful soul.

JEREMIAH 31:25

FEBRUARY 19

There is a spirit in man: and the inspiration of the Almighty giveth them understanding.

Job 32:8

NOVEMBER 12

Pleasant words are as an honeycomb, sweet to the soul, and health to the bones.

PROVERBS 16:24

FEBRUARY 20

Praise ye the Lord. Praise, O ye servants of the Lord, praise the name of the Lord. Blessed be the name of the Lord from this time forth and for evermore. From the rising of the sun unto the going down of the same the Lord's name is to be praised.

PSALM 113:1–3

NOVEMBER 11

For the love of Christ constraineth us; because we thus judge, that if one died for all, then were all dead: And that he died for all, that they which live should not henceforth live unto themselves, but unto him which died for them, and rose again.

2 Corinthians 5:14–15

FEBRUARY 21

Where two or three are gathered together in my name, there am I in the midst of them.

MATTHEW 18:20

NOVEMBER 10

Yet the Lord will command his lovingkindness in the daytime, and in the night his song shall be with me, and my prayer unto the God of my life.

PSALM 42:8

FEBRUARY 22

Every good gift and every perfect gift is from above, and cometh down from the Father of lights, with whom is no variableness, neither shadow of turning.

JAMES 1:17

NOVEMBER 9

In the time of trouble he shall hide me in his pavilion: in the secret of his tabernacle shall he hide me; he shall set me up upon a rock.

PSALM 27:5

FEBRUARY 23

I will go before thee, and make the crooked places straight: I will break in pieces the gates of brass, and cut in sunder the bars of iron: And I will give thee the treasures of darkness, and hidden riches of secret places, that thou mayest know that I, the Lord, which call thee by thy name, am the God of Israel.

Isaiah 45:2–3

NOVEMBER 8

Thou art my hiding place and my shield: I hope in thy word.... Therefore I love thy testimonies.

PSALM 119:114,119

FEBRUARY 24

O Lord, thou hast searched me, and known me. Thou knowest my downsitting and mine uprising, thou understandest my thought afar off.

PSALM 139:1–2

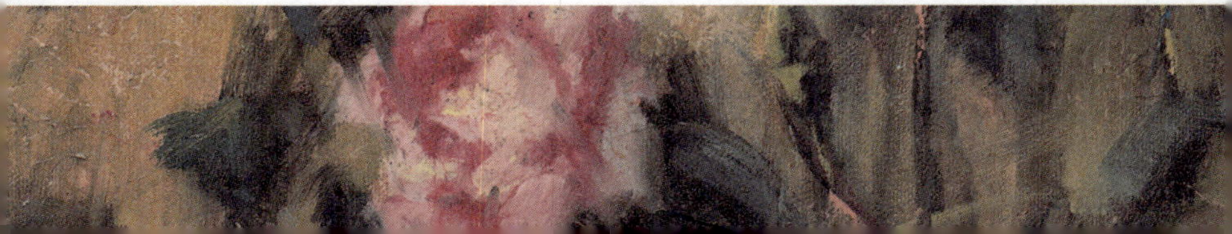

NOVEMBER 7

But I will sing of thy power; yea, I will sing aloud of thy mercy in the morning: for thou hast been my defence and refuge in the day of my trouble. Unto thee, O my strength, will I sing: for God is my defence, and the God of my mercy.

PSALM 59:16–17

FEBRUARY 25

He shall cover thee with his feathers, and under his wings shalt thou trust: his truth shall be thy shield and buckler. Thou shalt not be afraid for the terror by night; nor for the arrow that flieth by day;

PSALM 91:4–5

NOVEMBER 6

And even to your old age I am he...: I have made, and I will bear; even I will carry, and will deliver you.

ISAIAH 46:4

FEBRUARY 26

But unto you that fear my name shall the Sun of righteousness arise with healing in his wings.

MALACHI 4:2

NOVEMBER 5

The Lord hath done great things for us; whereof we are glad.

Psalm 126:3

FEBRUARY 27

We are more than conquerors through him that loved us. For I am persuaded, that neither death, nor life, nor angels, nor principalities, nor powers, nor things present, nor things to come, nor height, nor depth, nor any other creature, shall be able to separate us from the love of God.

ROMANS 8:37–39

NOVEMBER 4

The Lord hath appeared of old unto me, saying, Yea, I have loved thee with an everlasting love: therefore with lovingkindness have I drawn thee.

JEREMIAH 31:3

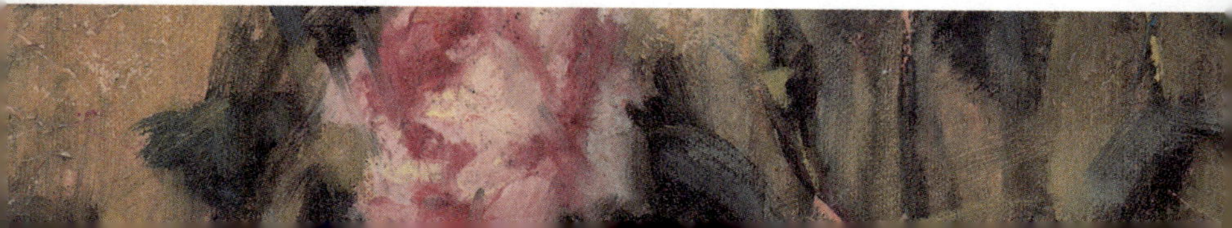

FEBRUARY 28

The Lord said, If ye had faith as a grain of mustard seed, ye might say unto this sycamine tree, Be thou plucked up by the root, and be thou planted in the sea; and it should obey you.

LUKE 17:6

NOVEMBER 3

But we believe that through the grace of the Lord Jesus Christ we shall be saved.

ACTS 15:11

FEBRUARY 29

Behold, I stand at the door, and knock: if any man hear my voice, and open the door, I will come in to him, and will sup with him, and he with me.

REVELATION 3:20

NOVEMBER 2

The Lord is righteous in all his ways, and holy in all his works. The Lord is nigh unto all them that call upon him, to all that call upon him in truth. He will fulfil the desire of them that fear him: he also will hear their cry, and will save them.

PSALM 145:17–19

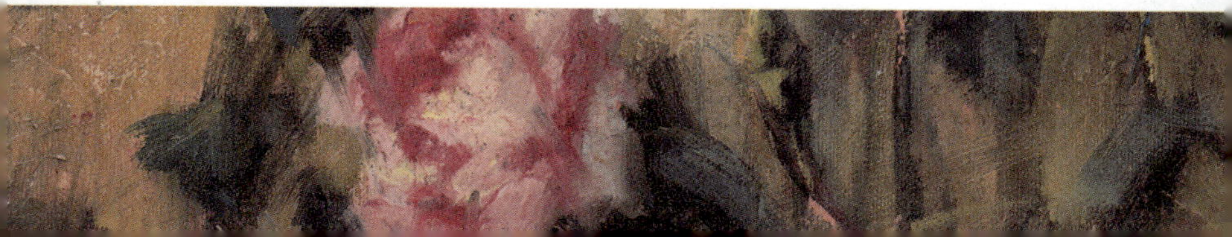

MARCH 1

The righteous cry, and the Lord delivereth them out of all their troubles.

PSALM 34:17

NOVEMBER 1

But now thus saith the Lord..., Fear not: for I have redeemed thee, I have called thee by thy name; thou art mine. When thou passest through the waters, I will be with thee; and through the rivers, they shall not overflow thee: when thou walkest through the fire, thou shalt not be burned.

ISAIAH 43:1–2

MARCH 2

God is a Spirit: and they that worship him must worship him in spirit and in truth.

JOHN 4:24

OCTOBER 31

For I have said, Mercy shall be built up for ever: thy faithfulness shalt thou establish in the very heavens.

PSALM 89:2

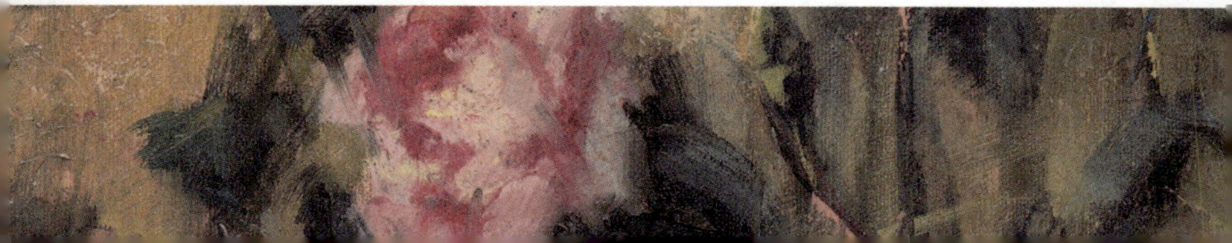

MARCH 3

Abide in me, and I in you. As the branch cannot bear fruit of itself, except it abide in the vine; no more can ye, except ye abide in me.

JOHN 15:4

OCTOBER 30

But thou, when thou prayest, enter into thy closet, and when thou hast shut thy door, pray to thy Father which is in secret; and thy Father which seeth in secret shall reward thee openly.

MATTHEW 6:6

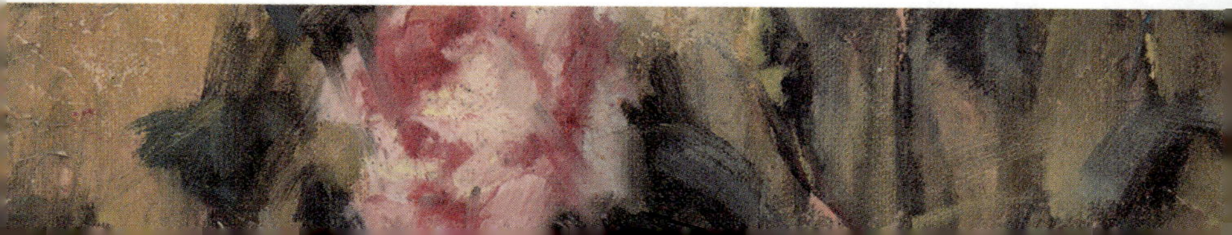

MARCH 4

If any man will come after me, let him deny himself, and take up his cross daily, and follow me. For whosoever will save his life shall lose it: but whosoever will lose his life for my sake, the same shall save it.

LUKE 9:23–24

OCTOBER 29

For the word of the Lord is right; and all his works are done in truth. He loveth righteousness and judgment: the earth is full of the goodness of the Lord. By the word of the Lord were the heavens made; and all the host of them by the breath of his mouth.

PSALM 33:4–6

MARCH 5

For God hath not given us the spirit of fear; but of power, and of love, and of a sound mind.

2 TIMOTHY 1:7

OCTOBER 28

My little children, let us not love in word, neither in tongue; but in deed and in truth.

1 John 3:18

MARCH 6

Not by might, nor by power, but by my spirit, saith the Lord of hosts.

ZECHARIAH 4:6

OCTOBER 27

Create in me a clean heart, O God;
and renew a right spirit within me.

PSALM 51:10

MARCH 7

Let them shout for joy, and be glad, that favour my righteous cause: yea, let them say continually, Let the Lord be magnified, which hath pleasure in the prosperity of his servant. And my tongue shall speak of thy righteousness and of thy praise all the day long.

PSALM 35:27–28

OCTOBER 26

And I will strengthen them in the Lord; and they shall walk up and down in his name, saith the Lord.

ZECHARIAH 10:12

MARCH 8

Though I speak with the tongues of men and of angels, and have not charity, I am become as sounding brass, or a tinkling cymbal. And though I have the gift of prophecy, and understand all mysteries, and all knowledge; and though I have all faith, so that I could remove mountains, and have not charity, I am nothing.

1 Corinthians 13:1–2

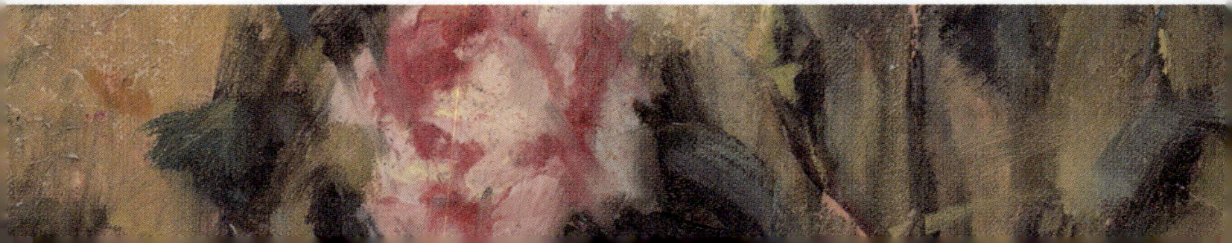

OCTOBER 25

And all these blessings shall come on thee, and overtake thee, if thou shalt hearken unto the voice of the Lord thy God.

DEUTERONOMY 28:2

MARCH 9

Pray without ceasing.

1 THESSALONIANS 5:17

OCTOBER 24

Lord, it is nothing with thee to help, whether with many, or with them that have no power: help us, O Lord our God; for we rest on thee, and in thy name we go against this multitude. O Lord, thou art our God; let not man prevail against thee.

2 Chronicles 14:11

MARCH 10

The heavens declare the glory of God; and the firmament sheweth his handywork. Day unto day uttereth speech, and night unto night sheweth knowledge. There is no speech nor language, where their voice is not heard.

PSALM 19:1-3

OCTOBER 23

The sacrifices of God are a broken spirit:
a broken and a contrite heart, O God,
thou wilt not despise.

PSALM 51:17

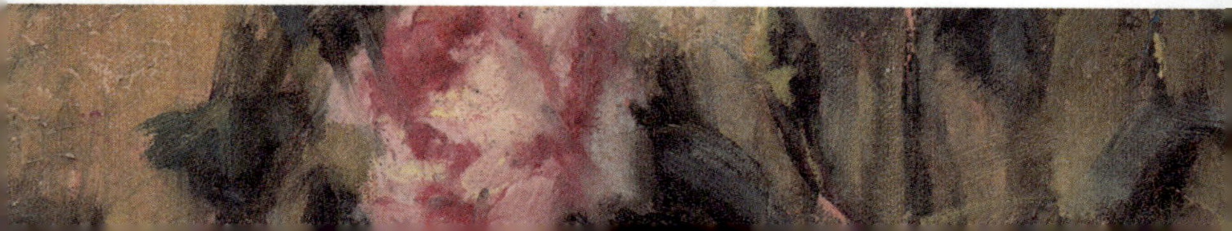

MARCH 11

Seek ye first the kingdom of God, and his righteousness; and all these things shall be added unto you. Take therefore no thought for the morrow: for the morrow shall take thought for the things of itself.

MATTHEW 6:33-34

OCTOBER 22

The Lord thy God in the midst of thee is mighty; he will save, he will rejoice over thee with joy; he will rest in his love, he will joy over thee with singing.

ZEPHANIAH 3:17

MARCH 12

Forget not all his benefits...who redeemeth thy life from destruction; who crowneth thee with lovingkindness and tender mercies; Who satisfieth thy mouth with good things; so that thy youth is renewed like the eagle's.

PSALM 103:2,4–5

OCTOBER 21

Give unto the Lord the glory due unto his name; worship the Lord in the beauty of holiness.

PSALM 29:2

MARCH 13

I the Lord thy God am a jealous God,... shewing mercy unto thousands of them that love me and keep my commandments.

DEUTERONOMY 5:9–10

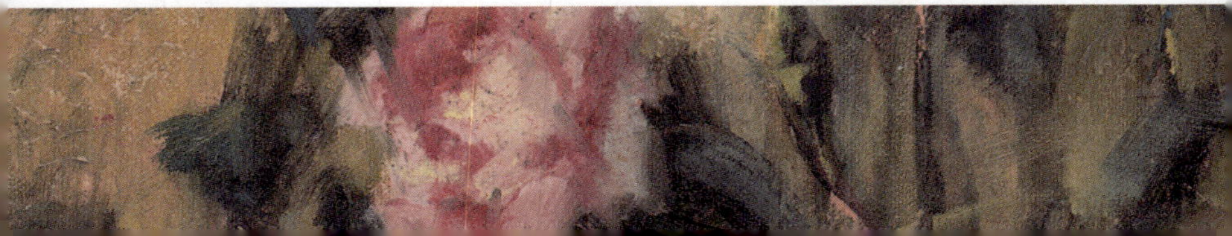

OCTOBER 20

O give thanks unto the Lord; for he is good; for his mercy endureth for ever.

1 Chronicles 16:34

MARCH 14

Finally, brethren, whatsoever things are true, whatsoever things are honest, whatsoever things are just, whatsoever things are pure, whatsoever things are lovely, whatsoever things are of good report; if there be any virtue, and if there be any praise, think on these things.

PHILIPPIANS 4:8

OCTOBER 19

For with thee is the fountain of life: in thy light shall we see light. O continue thy lovingkindness unto them that know thee; and thy righteousness to the upright in heart.

PSALM 36:9–10

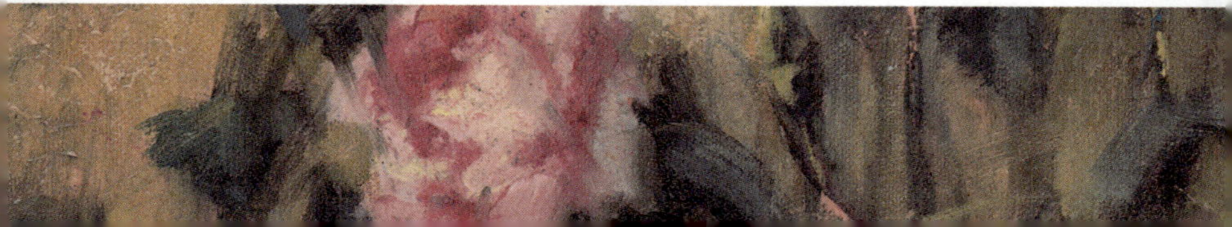

MARCH 15

For thus saith the Lord God, the Holy One of Israel; In returning and rest shall ye be saved; in quietness and in confidence shall be your strength.

ISAIAH 30:15

OCTOBER 18

These things have I spoken unto you, that my joy might remain in you, and that your joy might be full. This is my commandment, That ye love one another, as I have loved you. Greater love hath no man than this, that a man lay down his life for his friends.

John 15:11-13

MARCH 16

This book of the law shall not depart out of thy mouth; but thou shalt meditate therein day and night, that thou mayest observe to do according to all that is written therein: for then thou shalt make thy way prosperous, and then thou shalt have good success.

JOSHUA 1:8

OCTOBER 17

And God is able to make all grace abound toward you; that ye, always having all sufficiency in all things, may abound to every good work.

2 Corinthians 9:8

MARCH 17

Some trust in chariots, and some in horses: but we will remember the name of the Lord our God. They are brought down and fallen: but we are risen, and stand upright.

PSALM 20:7-8

OCTOBER 16

Whatsoever thy hand findeth to do, do it with thy might.

ECCLESIASTES 9:10

MARCH 18

I delight to do thy will, O my God:
yea, thy law is within my heart.

PSALM 40:8

OCTOBER 15

Set your affection on things above, not on things on the earth.

COLOSSIANS 3:2

MARCH 19

I can do all things through Christ which strengtheneth me.

PHILIPPIANS 4:13

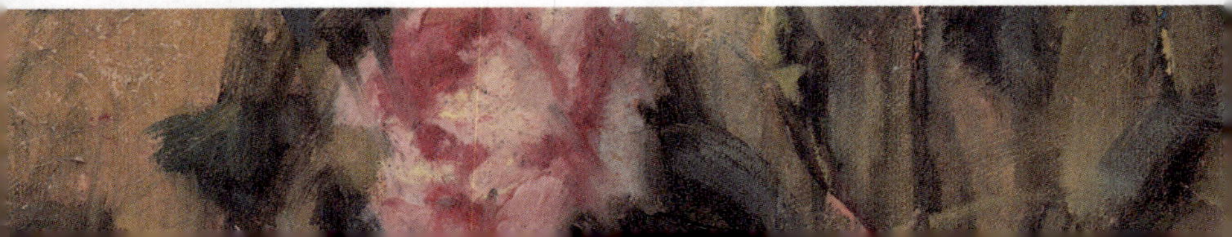

OCTOBER 14

And I will betroth thee unto me for ever; yea, I will betroth thee unto me in righteousness, and in judgment, and in lovingkindness, and in mercies. I will even betroth thee unto me in faithfulness: and thou shalt know the Lord.

Hosea 2:19–20

MARCH 20

Ye call upon me, and ye shall go and pray unto me, and I will hearken unto you. And ye shall seek me, and find me, when ye shall search for me with all your heart. And I will be found of you, saith the Lord.

JEREMIAH 29:12–14

OCTOBER 13

The Lord is nigh unto them that are of a broken heart; and saveth such as be of a contrite spirit.

PSALM 34:18

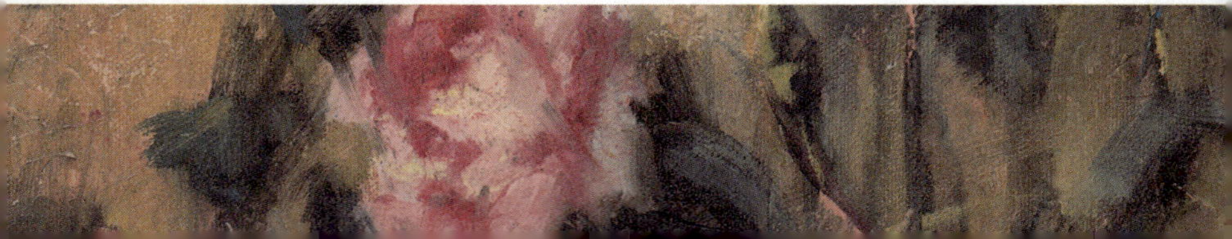

MARCH 21

The Lord seeth not as man seeth;
for man looketh on the outward appearance,
but the Lord looketh on the heart.

1 SAMUEL 16:7

OCTOBER 12

Mercy unto you, and peace,
and love, be multiplied.

JUDE 1:2

MARCH 22

Verily, verily, I say unto you, He that believeth on me, the works that I do shall he do also; and greater works than these shall he do; because I go unto my Father. And whatsoever ye shall ask in my name, that will I do, that the Father may be glorified in the Son.

JOHN 14:12–13

OCTOBER 11

Call unto me, and I will answer thee, and shew thee great and mighty things, which thou knowest not.

Jeremiah 33:3

MARCH 23

He that hath my commandments, and keepeth them, he it is that loveth me: and he that loveth me shall be loved of my Father, and I will love him, and will manifest myself to him.

JOHN 14:21

OCTOBER 10

Blessed are they which are persecuted for righteousness' sake: for theirs is the kingdom of heaven.

MATTHEW 5:10

MARCH 24

Rejoice in the Lord alway:
and again I say, Rejoice.

PHILIPPIANS 4:4

OCTOBER 9

Bless the Lord, O my soul. O Lord my God, thou art very great; thou art clothed with honour and majesty.

PSALM 104:1

MARCH 25

I am crucified with Christ: nevertheless I live; yet not I, but Christ liveth in me: and the life which I now live in the flesh I live by the faith of the Son of God, who loved me, and gave himself for me.

GALATIANS 2:20

OCTOBER 8

Nevertheless we, according to his promise, look for new heavens and a new earth, wherein dwelleth righteousness.

2 Peter 3:13

MARCH 26

For God so loved the world, that he gave his only begotten Son, that whosoever believeth in him should not perish, but have everlasting life.

JOHN 3:16

OCTOBER 7

The Lord shall preserve thy going out and thy coming in from this time forth, and even for evermore.

Psalm 121:8

MARCH 27

There remaineth therefore a rest to the people of God. For he that is entered into his rest, he also hath ceased from his own works, as God did from his. Let us labour therefore to enter into that rest, lest any man fall after the same example of unbelief.

HEBREWS 4:9–11

OCTOBER 6

Search me, O God, and know my heart: try me, and know my thoughts: And see if there be any wicked way in me, and lead me in the way everlasting.

PSALM 139:23-24

MARCH 28

Honour and majesty are before him: strength and beauty are in his sanctuary.

PSALM 96:6

OCTOBER 5

The Lord is my rock, and my fortress, and my deliverer; my God, my strength, in whom I will trust; my buckler, and the horn of my salvation, and my high tower.

PSALM 18:2

MARCH 29

Thine ears shall hear a word behind thee, saying, This is the way, walk ye in it, when ye turn to the right hand, and when ye turn to the left.

Isaiah 30:21

OCTOBER 4

He hath chosen us in him before the foundation of the world, that we should be holy and without blame before him in love: Having predestinated us unto the adoption of children by Jesus Christ to himself, according to the good pleasure of his will.

EPHESIANS 1:4-6

MARCH 30

My grace is sufficient for thee: for my strength is made perfect in weakness.... Therefore I take pleasure in infirmities, in reproaches, in necessities, in persecutions, in distresses for Christ's sake: for when I am weak, then am I strong.

2 Corinthians 12:9–10

OCTOBER 3

But the mercy of the Lord is from everlasting to everlasting upon them that fear him, and his righteousness unto children's children.

PSALM 103:17

MARCH 31

And we have known and believed the love that God hath to us. God is love; and he that dwelleth in love dwelleth in God, and God in him.

1 John 4:16

OCTOBER 2

Herein is love, not that we loved God, but that he loved us, and sent his Son to be the propitiation for our sins. Beloved, if God so loved us, we ought also to love one another.

1 John 4:10–11

APRIL 1

If ye continue in my word, then are ye my disciples indeed; And ye shall know the truth, and the truth shall make you free.

JOHN 8:31-32

OCTOBER 1

But lay up for yourselves treasures in heaven, where neither moth nor rust doth corrupt, and where thieves do not break through nor steal: For where your treasure is, there will your heart be also.

Matthew 6:20–21

APRIL 2

Love worketh no ill to his neighbour: therefore love is the fulfilling of the law.

ROMANS 13:10

SEPTEMBER 30

And Jesus looking upon them saith, With men it is impossible, but not with God: for with God all things are possible.

MARK 10:27

APRIL 3

For we have not an high priest which cannot be touched with the feeling of our infirmities; but was in all points tempted like as we are, yet without sin.

Hebrews 4:15

SEPTEMBER 29

Many sorrows shall be to the wicked: but he that trusteth in the Lord, mercy shall compass him about.

Psalm 32:10

APRIL 4

Serve the Lord with gladness: come before his presence with singing. Know ye that the Lord he is God: it is he that hath made us...; we are his people, and the sheep of his pasture. Enter into his gates with thanksgiving, and into his courts with praise.

PSALM 100:2-4

SEPTEMBER 28

Forbearing one another, and forgiving one another, if any man have a quarrel against any: even as Christ forgave you, so also do ye.

COLOSSIANS 3:13

APRIL 5

My sheep hear my voice, and I know them, and they follow me: And I give unto them eternal life; and they shall never perish, neither shall any man pluck them out of my hand. My Father, which gave them me, is greater than all; and no man is able to pluck them out of my Father's hand.

JOHN 10:27–29

SEPTEMBER 27

The God of my mercy shall prevent me: God shall let me see my desire upon mine enemies.

PSALM 59:10

APRIL 6

Will I not forget thee. Behold, I have graven thee upon the palms of my hands.

ISAIAH 49:15–16

SEPTEMBER 26

O the depth of the riches both of the wisdom and knowledge of God! how unsearchable are his judgments, and his ways past finding out! For who hath known the mind of the Lord? or who hath been his counsellor?

Romans 11:33–34

APRIL 7

I can of mine own self do nothing: as I hear, I judge: and my judgment is just; because I seek not mine own will, but the will of the Father which hath sent me.

JOHN 5:30

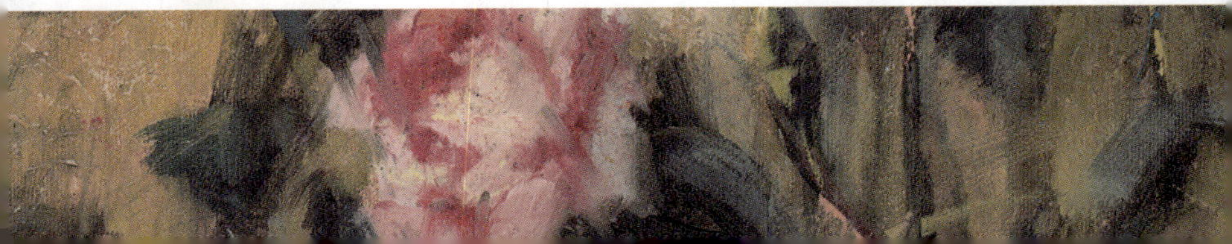

SEPTEMBER 25

For the eyes of the Lord are over the righteous, and his ears are open unto their prayers: but the face of the Lord is against them that do evil.

1 PETER 3:12

APRIL 8

And he said, My presence shall go with thee, and I will give thee rest.

EXODUS 33:14

SEPTEMBER 24

Thou art worthy, O Lord, to receive glory and honour and power: for thou hast created all things, and for thy pleasure they are and were created.

REVELATION 4:11

APRIL 9

Ask, and it shall be given you; seek, and ye shall find; knock, and it shall be opened unto you. For every one that asketh receiveth; and he that seeketh findeth; and to him that knocketh it shall be opened.

LUKE 11:9–10

SEPTEMBER 23

But we have this treasure in earthen vessels, that the excellency of the power may be of God, and not of us.

2 CORINTHIANS 4:7

APRIL 10

For my thoughts are not your thoughts, neither are your ways my ways, saith the Lord. For as the heavens are higher than the earth, so are my ways higher than your ways, and my thoughts than your thoughts.

ISAIAH 55:8-9

SEPTEMBER 22

The Lord our God is one Lord: And thou shalt love the Lord thy God with all thy heart, and with all thy soul, and with all thy mind, and with all thy strength: this is the first commandment.

MARK 12:29–30

APRIL 11

And be ye kind one to another, tenderhearted, forgiving one another, even as God for Christ's sake hath forgiven you.

EPHESIANS 4:32

SEPTEMBER 21

But let it be the hidden man of the heart, in that which is not corruptible, even the ornament of a meek and quiet spirit, which is in the sight of God of great price.

1 PETER 3:4

APRIL 12

Blessed is the man that walketh not in the counsel of the ungodly, nor standeth in the way of sinners, nor sitteth in the seat of the scornful. But his delight is in the law of the Lord; and in his law doth he meditate day and night.

PSALM 1:1–2

SEPTEMBER 20

And I heard as it were the voice of a great multitude, and as the voice of many waters, and as the voice of mighty thunderings, saying, Alleluia: for the Lord God omnipotent reigneth. Let us be glad and rejoice, and give honour to him: for the marriage of the Lamb is come.

REVELATION 19:6-7

APRIL 13

The Lord bless thee, and keep thee: The Lord make his face shine upon thee, and be gracious unto thee: The Lord lift up his countenance upon thee, and give thee peace.

NUMBERS 6:24–26

SEPTEMBER 19

As for God, his way is perfect: the word of the Lord is tried: he is a buckler to all those that trust in him.

PSALM 18:30

APRIL 14

Bless the Lord, O my soul: and all that is within me, bless his holy name. Bless the Lord, O my soul, and forget not all his benefits: Who forgiveth all thine iniquities; who healeth all thy diseases.

PSALM 103:1-3

SEPTEMBER 18

The same Lord over all is rich unto all that call upon him.

ROMANS 10:12

APRIL 15

Hear me when I call, O God of my righteousness: thou hast enlarged me when I was in distress; have mercy upon me, and hear my prayer.

Psalm 4:1

SEPTEMBER 17

And I will restore to you the years that the locust hath eaten.... And ye shall eat in plenty, and be satisfied, and praise the name of the Lord your God, that hath dealt wondrously with you.

JOEL 2:25-26

APRIL 16

There is no fear in love; but perfect love casteth out fear: because fear hath torment. He that feareth is not made perfect in love.

1 John 4:18

SEPTEMBER 16

Withhold not thou thy tender mercies from me, O Lord: let thy lovingkindness and thy truth continually preserve me.

Psalm 40:11

APRIL 17

Behold, as the eyes of servants look unto the hand of their masters, and as the eyes of a maiden unto the hand of her mistress; so our eyes wait upon the Lord our God, until that he have mercy upon us.

PSALM 123:2

SEPTEMBER 15

Now the God of peace...make you perfect in every good work to do his will, working in you that which is wellpleasing in his sight, through Jesus Christ; to whom be glory for ever and ever. Amen.

HEBREWS 13:20–21

APRIL 18

For it is God which worketh in you both
to will and to do of his good pleasure.

PHILIPPIANS 2:13

SEPTEMBER 14

Then shall we know, if we follow on to know the Lord: his going forth is prepared as the morning; and he shall come unto us as the rain, as the latter and former rain unto the earth.

HOSEA 6:3

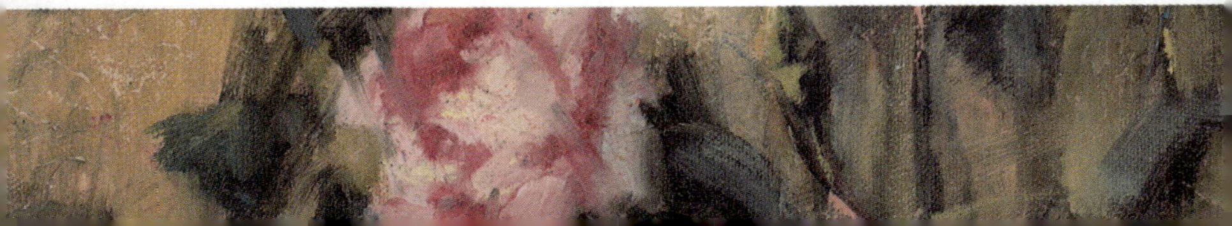

APRIL 19

Thou hast beset me behind and before, and laid thine hand upon me. Such knowledge is too wonderful for me; it is high, I cannot attain unto it.

PSALM 139:5-6

SEPTEMBER 13

No man hath seen God at any time.
If we love one another, God dwelleth in us,
and his love is perfected in us.

1 JOHN 4:12

APRIL 20

Humble yourselves therefore under the mighty hand of God, that he may exalt you in due time.

1 PETER 5:6

SEPTEMBER 12

If my people, which are called by my name,
shall humble themselves, and pray, and seek
my face, and turn from their wicked ways; then
will I hear from heaven, and will forgive their sin,
and will heal their land.

2 Chronicles 7:14

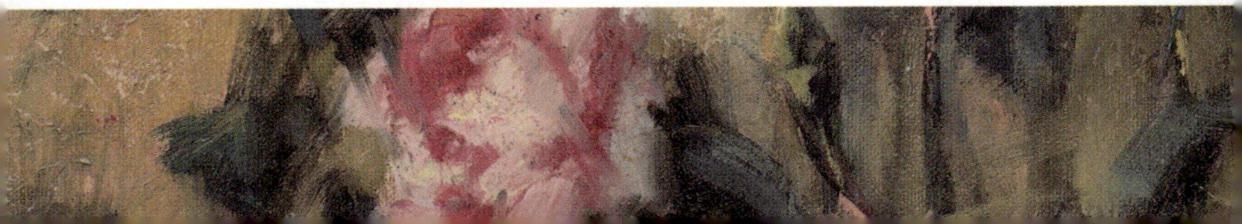

APRIL 21

Thus saith the Lord, Stand ye in the ways,
and see, and ask for the old paths,
where is the good way, and walk therein,
and ye shall find rest for your souls.

JEREMIAH 6:16

SEPTEMBER 11

For his anger endureth but a moment; in his favour is life: weeping may endure for a night, but joy cometh in the morning.

PSALM 30:5

APRIL 22

But thou, O Lord, art a shield for me; my glory, and the lifter up of mine head. I cried unto the Lord with my voice, and he heard me out of his holy hill. I laid me down and slept; I awaked; for the Lord sustained me.

PSALM 3:3–5

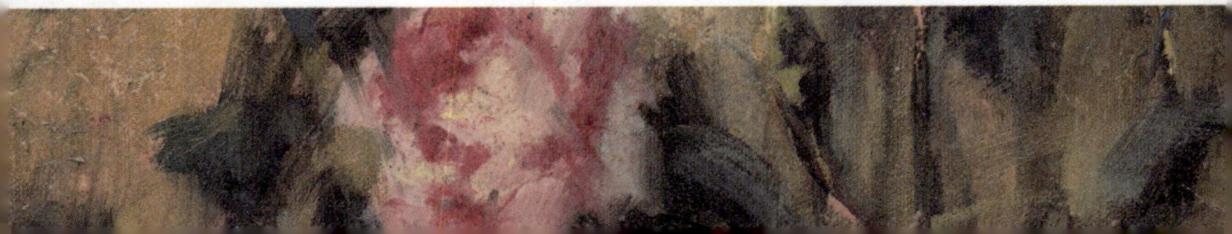

SEPTEMBER 10

Ask ye of the Lord rain in the time of the latter rain; so the Lord shall make bright clouds, and give them showers of rain, to every one grass in the field.

ZECHARIAH 10:1

APRIL 23

Again I say unto you, That if two of you shall agree on earth as touching any thing that they shall ask, it shall be done for them of my Father which is in heaven.

MATTHEW 18:19

SEPTEMBER 9

Where is boasting then? It is excluded. By what law? of works? Nay: but by the law of faith. Therefore we conclude that a man is justified by faith without the deeds of the law.

ROMANS 3:27–28

APRIL 24

The eternal God is thy refuge, and underneath are the everlasting arms.

Deuteronomy 33:27

SEPTEMBER 8

And the Lord, he it is that doth go before thee; he will be with thee, he will not fail thee, neither forsake thee: fear not, neither be dismayed.

DEUTERONOMY 31:8

APRIL 25

Therefore I say unto you, What things soever ye desire, when ye pray, believe that ye receive them, and ye shall have them.

MARK 11:24

SEPTEMBER 7

Now the God of patience and consolation grant you to be likeminded one toward another according to Christ Jesus.

ROMANS 15:5

APRIL 26

I will not be afraid of ten thousands of people, that have set themselves against me round about. Arise, O Lord; save me.... Salvation belongeth unto the Lord: thy blessing is upon thy people.

PSALM 3:6–8

SEPTEMBER 6

God that made the world and all things therein, seeing that he is Lord of heaven and earth, dwelleth not in temples made with hands; Neither is worshipped with men's hands, as though he needed any thing, seeing he giveth to all life, and breath, and all things.

ACTS 17:25

APRIL 27

*N*ot that we are sufficient of ourselves
to think any thing as of ourselves;
but our sufficiency is of God.

2 CORINTHIANS 3:5

SEPTEMBER 5

Trust ye in the Lord for ever: for in the Lord Jehovah is everlasting strength.

ISAIAH 26:4

APRIL 28

If ye have faith as a grain of mustard seed, ye shall say unto this mountain, Remove hence to yonder place; and it shall remove; and nothing shall be impossible unto you.

MATTHEW 17:20

SEPTEMBER 4

And above all things have fervent charity among yourselves: for charity shall cover the multitude of sins.

1 PETER 4:8

APRIL 29

As ye have therefore received Christ Jesus the Lord, so walk ye in him: Rooted and built up in him, and stablished in the faith, as ye have been taught, abounding therein with thanksgiving.

COLOSSIANS 2:6-7

SEPTEMBER 3

The earth is the Lord's, and the fulness thereof; the world, and they that dwell therein. For he hath founded it upon the seas, and established it upon the floods.

PSALM 24:1–2

APRIL 30

For, lo, the winter is past, the rain is over and gone; The flowers appear on the earth; the time of the singing of birds is come, and the voice of the turtle is heard in our land.

SONG OF SOLOMON 2:11-12

SEPTEMBER 2

Thou in thy mercy hast led forth the people which thou hast redeemed: thou hast guided them in thy strength unto thy holy habitation.

Exodus 15:13

MAY 1

And after the wind an earthquake; but the Lord was not in the earthquake: And after the earthquake a fire; but the Lord was not in the fire: and after the fire a still small voice.

1 Kings 19:11-12

SEPTEMBER 1

Grace and peace be multiplied unto you through the knowledge of God, and of Jesus our Lord.

2 Peter 1:2

MAY 2

But my God shall supply all your need according to his riches in glory by Christ Jesus.

PHILIPPIANS 4:19

AUGUST 31

The Lord is good, a strong hold in the day of trouble; and he knoweth them that trust in him.

NAHUM 1:7

MAY 3

And let the beauty of the Lord our God be upon us: and establish thou the work of our hands upon us; yea, the work of our hands establish thou it.

PSALM 90:17

AUGUST 30

Thine, O Lord, is the greatness, and the power, and the glory, and the victory, and the majesty: for all that is in the heaven and in the earth is thine; thine is the kingdom, O Lord, and thou art exalted as head above all.

1 CHRONICLES 29:11

MAY 4

These things I have spoken unto you, that in me ye might have peace. In the world ye shall have tribulation: but be of good cheer; I have overcome the world.

JOHN 16:33

AUGUST 29

Thou shalt not bow down thyself to them, nor serve them: for I the LORD thy God am a jealous God.... And shewing mercy unto thousands of them that love me, and keep my commandments.

EXODUS 20:5-6

MAY 5

I will lift up mine eyes unto the hills, from whence cometh my help. My help cometh from the Lord, which made heaven and earth.

Psalm 121:1-2

AUGUST 28

Thy kingdom is an everlasting kingdom, and thy dominion endureth throughout all generations.

PSALM 145:13

MAY 6

Take my yoke upon you, and learn of me; for I am meek and lowly in heart: and ye shall find rest unto your souls. For my yoke is easy, and my burden is light.

MATTHEW 11:29-30

AUGUST 27

With everlasting kindness will I have mercy on thee, saith the Lord thy Redeemer.

ISAIAH 54:8

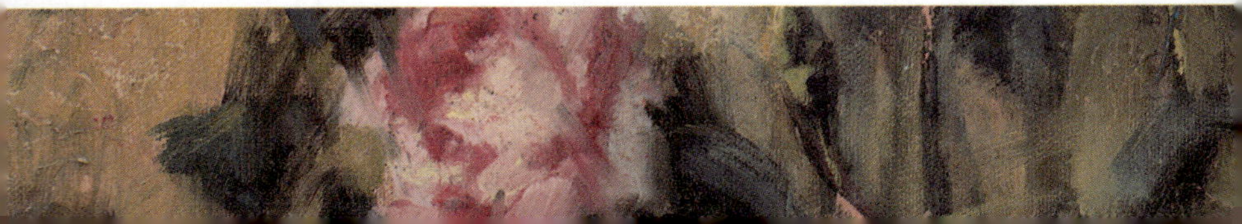

MAY 7

Therefore being justified by faith, we have peace with God through our Lord Jesus Christ: By whom also we have access by faith into this grace wherein we stand, and rejoice in hope of the glory of God.

ROMANS 5:1–2

AUGUST 26

Seek the Lord and his strength,
seek his face continually.

1 Chronicles 16:11

MAY 8

There is therefore now no condemnation to them which are in Christ Jesus, who walk not after the flesh, but after the Spirit.

ROMANS 8:1

AUGUST 25

Shew me thy ways, O Lord; teach me thy paths. Lead me in thy truth, and teach me: for thou art the God of my salvation; on thee do I wait all the day.

PSALM 25:4–5

MAY 9

Give ear to my words, O Lord, consider my meditation. Hearken unto the voice of my cry, my King, and my God: for unto thee will I pray. My voice shalt thou hear in the morning, O Lord; in the morning will I direct my prayer unto thee, and will look up.

PSALM 5:1-3

AUGUST 24

O come, let us worship and bow down:
let us kneel before the Lord our maker. For he is
our God; and we are the people of his pasture,
and the sheep of his hand.

PSALM 95:6–7

MAY 10

Behold, he that keepeth Israel shall neither slumber nor sleep. The Lord is thy keeper: the Lord is thy shade upon thy right hand.

PSALM 121:4-5

AUGUST 23

For since the beginning of the world men have not heard, nor perceived by the ear, neither hath the eye seen, O God, beside thee, what he hath prepared for him that waiteth for him.

Isaiah 64:4

MAY 11

Being confident of this very thing, that he which hath begun a good work in you will perform it until the day of Jesus Christ.

PHILIPPIANS 1:6

AUGUST 22

Now unto the King eternal, immortal, invisible, the only wise God, be honour and glory for ever and ever. Amen.

1 Timothy 1:17

MAY 12

Thou art my hiding place; thou shalt preserve me from trouble; thou shalt compass me about with songs of deliverance.

PSALM 32:7

AUGUST 21

Put on therefore, as the elect of God, holy and beloved, bowels of mercies, kindness, humbleness of mind, meekness, longsuffering.

COLOSSIANS 3:12

MAY 13

The Lord is my shepherd; I shall not want.
He maketh me to lie down in green pastures:
he leadeth me beside the still waters.

PSALM 23:1-2

AUGUST 20

For God giveth to a man that is good in his sight wisdom, and knowledge, and joy.

ECCLESIASTES 2:26

MAY 14

Keep me as the apple of the eye, hide me under the shadow of thy wings.

Psalm 17:8

AUGUST 19

Thy word is very pure: therefore thy servant loveth it.

Psalm 119:140

MAY 15

A man's heart deviseth his way: but the Lord directeth his steps.

PROVERBS 16:9

AUGUST 18

But let him that glorieth glory in this, that he understandeth and knoweth me, that I am the Lord which exercise lovingkindness, judgment, and righteousness, in the earth: for in these things I delight, saith the Lord.

JEREMIAH 9:24

MAY 16

And I will walk among you, and will be your God, and ye shall be my people.

LEVITICUS 26:12

AUGUST 17

His divine power hath given unto us all things that pertain unto life and godliness, through the knowledge of him that hath called us to glory and virtue.

2 PETER 1:3

MAY 17

A word fitly spoken is like apples of gold in pictures of silver. As an earring of gold, and an ornament of fine gold, so is a wise reprover upon an obedient ear.

PROVERBS 25:11–12

AUGUST 16

Thou hast covered me in my mother's womb.
I will praise thee; for I am fearfully and wonderfully
made: marvellous are thy works; and that my
soul knoweth right well.

PSALM 139:13–14

MAY 18

For God sent not his Son into the world to condemn the world; but that the world through him might be saved.

JOHN 3:17

AUGUST 15

When I consider thy heavens, the work of thy fingers, the moon and the stars, which thou hast ordained.... O Lord our Lord, how excellent is thy name in all the earth!

PSALM 8:3,9

MAY 19

Oh how great is thy goodness, which thou hast laid up for them that fear thee; which thou hast wrought for them that trust in thee before the sons of men!

PSALM 31:19

AUGUST 14

As every man hath received the gift, even so minister the same one to another, as good stewards of the manifold grace of God.

1 PETER 4:10

MAY 20

Whosoever drinketh of this water shall thirst again: But whosoever drinketh of the water that I shall give him shall never thirst; but the water that I shall give him shall be in him a well of water springing up into everlasting life.

JOHN 4:13–14

AUGUST 13

Blessed be the God and Father of our Lord Jesus Christ, who hath blessed us with all spiritual blessings in heavenly places in Christ.

EPHESIANS 1:3

MAY 21

Unto thee, O God, do we give thanks, unto thee do we give thanks: for that thy name is near thy wondrous works declare.

Psalm 75:1

AUGUST 12

My soul followeth hard after thee:
thy right hand upholdeth me.

PSALM 63:8

MAY 22

As far as the east is from the west, so far hath he removed our transgressions from us.

PSALM 103:12

AUGUST 11

Be not ye therefore like unto them: for your Father knoweth what things ye have need of, before ye ask him.

MATTHEW 6:8

MAY 23

For ye shall go out with joy, and be led forth with peace: the mountains and the hills shall break forth before you into singing, and all the trees of the field shall clap their hands.

ISAIAH 55:12

AUGUST 10

As the hart panteth after the water brooks, so panteth my soul after thee, O God.

PSALM 42:1

MAY 24

Therefore if any man be in Christ, he is a new creature: old things are passed away; behold, all things are become new.

2 Corinthians 5:17

AUGUST 9

Thou preparest a table before me in the presence of mine enemies: thou anointest my head with oil; my cup runneth over. Surely goodness and mercy shall follow me all the days of my life: and I will dwell in the house of the Lord for ever.

PSALM 23:5-6

MAY 25

The Lord God is my strength, and he will make my feet like hinds' feet, and he will make me to walk upon mine high places.

HABAKKUK 3:19

AUGUST 8

Now our Lord Jesus Christ himself, and God, even our Father, which hath loved us, and hath given us everlasting consolation and good hope through grace, Comfort your hearts, and stablish you in every good word and work.

2 THESSALONIANS 2:16–17

MAY 26

In God will I praise his word: in the Lord will I praise his word. In God have I put my trust: I will not be afraid what man can do unto me.

PSALM 56:10–11

AUGUST 7

Now the God of hope fill you with all joy and peace in believing, that ye may abound in hope, through the power of the Holy Ghost.

ROMANS 15:13

MAY 27

If any man serve me, let him follow me; and where I am, there shall also my servant be: if any man serve me, him will my Father honour.

John 12:26

AUGUST 6

Thou wilt keep him in perfect peace, whose mind is stayed on thee: because he trusteth in thee.

ISAIAH 26:3

MAY 28

The name of the Lord is a strong tower: the righteous runneth into it, and is safe.

PROVERBS 18:10

AUGUST 5

And whatsoever ye do in word or deed, do all in the name of the Lord Jesus, giving thanks to God and the Father by him.

COLOSSIANS 3:17

MAY 29

And be not conformed to this world: but be ye transformed by the renewing of your mind, that ye may prove what is that good, and acceptable, and perfect, will of God.

ROMANS 12:2

AUGUST 4

But the wisdom that is from above is first pure, then peaceable, gentle, and easy to be intreated, full of mercy and good fruits, without partiality, and without hypocrisy.

JAMES 3:17

MAY 30

As the Father hath loved me, so have I loved you: continue ye in my love. If ye keep my commandments, ye shall abide in my love; even as I have kept my Father's commandments, and abide in his love.

John 15:9-10

AUGUST 3

Like as a father pitieth his children, so the Lord pitieth them that fear him. For he knoweth our frame; he remembereth that we are dust. As for man, his days are as grass: as a flower of the field, so he flourisheth.

PSALM 103:13–15

MAY 31

Thou wilt shew me the path of life: in thy presence is fulness of joy; at thy right hand there are pleasures for evermore.

Psalm 16:11

AUGUST 2

But he knoweth the way that I take: when he hath tried me, I shall come forth as gold.

Job 23:10

JUNE 1

For the Lord is good; his mercy is everlasting; and his truth endureth to all generations.

PSALM 100:5

AUGUST 1

But I say unto you, Love your enemies, bless them that curse you, do good to them that hate you, and pray for them which despitefully use you, and persecute you.

MATTHEW 5:44

JUNE 2

One thing have I desired of the Lord, that will I seek after; that I may dwell in the house of the Lord all the days of my life, to behold the beauty of the Lord, and to enquire in his temple.

Psalm 27:4

JULY 31

And the Lord shall guide thee continually, and satisfy thy soul in drought, and make fat thy bones: and thou shalt be like a watered garden, and like a spring of water, whose waters fail not.

ISAIAH 58:11

JUNE 3

Hast thou not known? hast thou not heard, that the everlasting God, the Lord, the Creator of the ends of the earth, fainteth not, neither is weary? there is no searching of his understanding.

ISAIAH 40:28

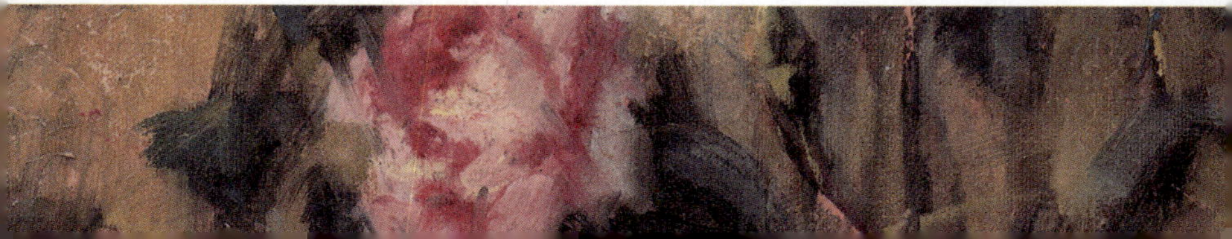

JULY 30

Behold, God is my salvation; I will trust, and not be afraid: for the Lord Jehovah is my strength and my song; he also is become my salvation.

Isaiah 12:2

JUNE 4

This is the confidence that we have in him, that, if we ask any thing according to his will, he heareth us: And if we know that he hear us, whatsoever we ask, we know that we have the petitions that we desired of him.

1 John 5:14–15

JULY 29

The Lord is not slack concerning his promise, as some men count slackness; but is longsuffering to us-ward, not willing that any should perish, but that all should come to repentance.

2 PETER 3:9

JUNE 5

With my whole heart have I sought thee: O let me not wander from thy commandments. Thy word have I hid in mine heart, that I might not sin against thee. Blessed art thou, O Lord: teach me thy statutes.

PSALM 119:10–12

JULY 28

For by grace are ye saved through faith; and that not of yourselves: it is the gift of God.

EPHESIANS 2:8

JUNE 6

Why art thou cast down, O my soul? and why art thou disquieted within me? hope in God: for I shall yet praise him, who is the health of my countenance, and my God.

PSALM 43:5

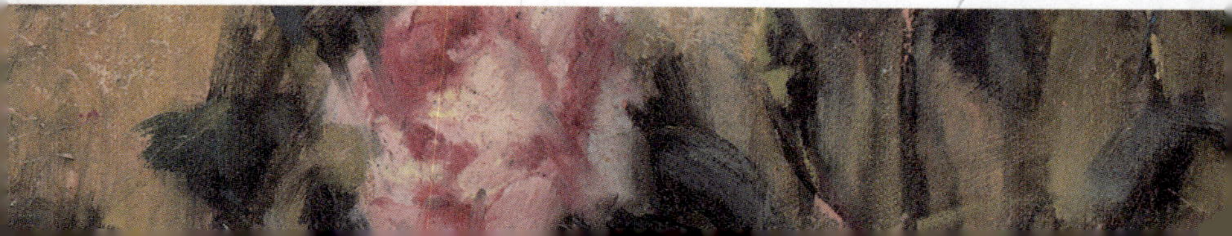

JULY 27

He hath made the earth by his power, he hath established the world by his wisdom, and hath stretched out the heavens by his discretion.

JEREMIAH 10:12

JUNE 7

Let your light so shine before men, that they may see your good works, and glorify your Father which is in heaven.

MATTHEW 5:16

JULY 26

Thy word is a lamp unto my feet,
and a light unto my path.

PSALM 119:105

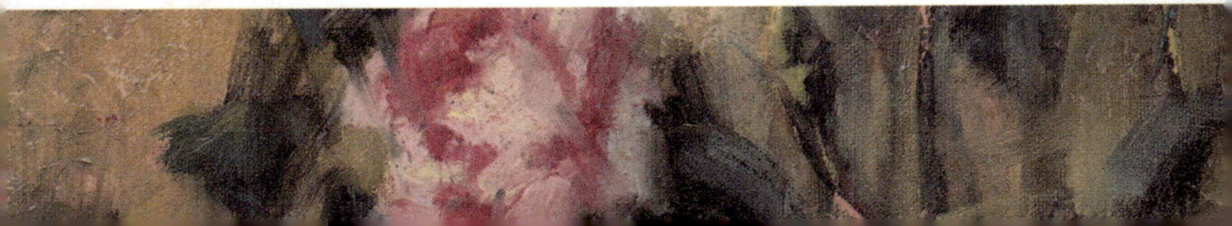

JUNE 8

He restoreth my soul: he leadeth me in the paths of righteousness for his name's sake. Yea, though I walk through the valley of the shadow of death, I will fear no evil: for thou art with me; thy rod and thy staff they comfort me.

Psalm 23:3-4

JULY 25

Truly my soul waiteth upon God: from him cometh my salvation.

PSALM 62:1

JUNE 9

And now abideth faith, hope, charity, these three; but the greatest of these is charity.

1 Corinthians 13:13

JULY 24

Blessed be God, even the Father of our Lord Jesus Christ, the Father of mercies, and the God of all comfort; Who comforteth us in all our tribulation, that we may be able to comfort them which are in any trouble, by the comfort wherewith we ourselves are comforted of God.

2 Corinthians 1:3–4

JUNE 10

And whatsoever ye do, do it heartily, as to the Lord, and not unto men; Knowing that of the Lord ye shall receive the reward of the inheritance: for ye serve the Lord Christ.

COLOSSIANS 3:23–24

JULY 23

Let us draw near with a true heart in full assurance of faith.... Let us hold fast the profession of our faith without wavering.

HEBREWS 10:22-23

JUNE 11

If ye abide in me, and my words abide in you, ye shall ask what ye will, and it shall be done unto you. Herein is my Father glorified, that ye bear much fruit.

JOHN 15:7–8

JULY 22

Whom have I in heaven but thee? and there is none upon earth that I desire beside thee. My flesh and my heart faileth: but God is the strength of my heart, and my portion for ever.

PSALM 73:25–26

JUNE 12

This is the day which the Lord hath made;
we will rejoice and be glad in it.

Psalm 118:24

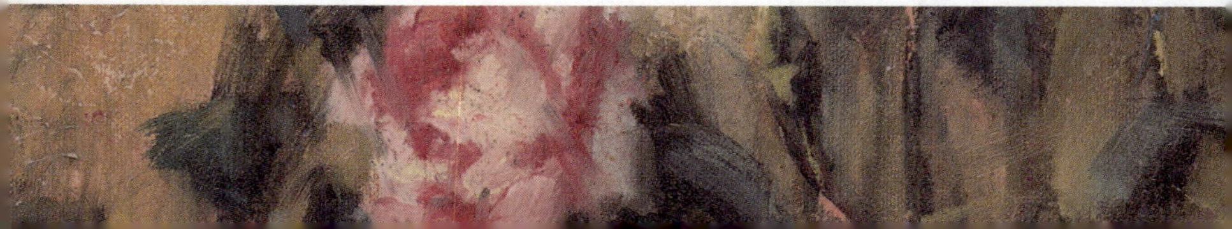

JULY 21

Humble yourselves therefore under the mighty hand of God, that he may exalt you in due time: Casting all your care upon him; for he careth for you.

1 Peter 5:6–7

JUNE 13

That they should seek the Lord.... For in him we live, and move, and have our being.

Acts 17:27–28

JULY 20

Let, I pray thee, thy merciful kindness be for my comfort, according to thy word unto thy servant.

PSALM 119:76

JUNE 14

There is that scattereth, and yet increaseth; and there is that withholdeth more than is meet, but it tendeth to poverty. The liberal soul shall be made fat: and he that watereth shall be watered also himself.

PROVERBS 11:24–25

JULY 19

Be thou exalted, O God, above the heavens; let thy glory be above all the earth.

PSALM 57:5

JUNE 15

But I have trusted in thy mercy; my heart shall rejoice in thy salvation. I will sing unto the Lord, because he hath dealt bountifully with me.

PSALM 13:5–6

JULY 18

Now faith is the substance of things hoped for, the evidence of things not seen.

HEBREWS 11:1

JUNE 16

O taste and see that the Lord is good: blessed is the man that trusteth in him. O fear the Lord, ye his saints: for there is no want to them that fear him.

PSALM 34:8-9

JULY 17

I will cause the shower to come down in his season; there shall be showers of blessing.

EZEKIEL 34:26

JUNE 17

And, behold, I am with thee, and will keep thee in all places whither thou goest.

GENESIS 28:15

JULY 16

But now, O Lord, thou art our father; we are the clay, and thou our potter; and we all are the work of thy hand.

Isaiah 64:8

JUNE 18

Behold, what manner of love the Father hath bestowed upon us, that we should be called the sons of God: therefore the world knoweth us not, because it knew him not.

1 John 3:1

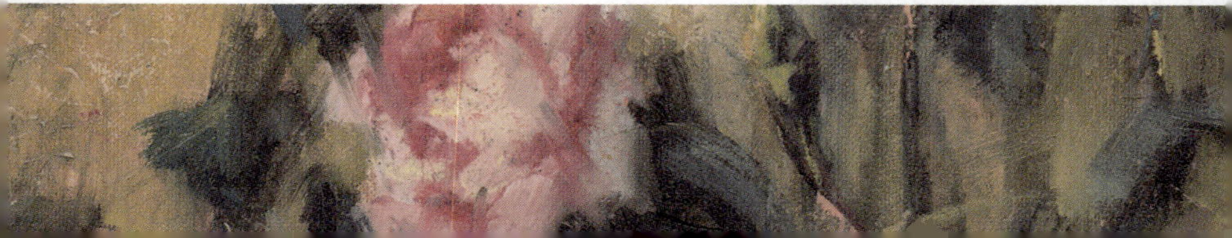

JULY 15

A new heart also will I give you, and a new spirit will I put within you: and I will take away the stony heart out of your flesh.... And I will put my spirit within you.

EZEKIEL 36:26–27

JUNE 19

While we look not at the things which are seen, but at the things which are not seen: for the things which are seen are temporal; but the things which are not seen are eternal.

2 CORINTHIANS 4:18

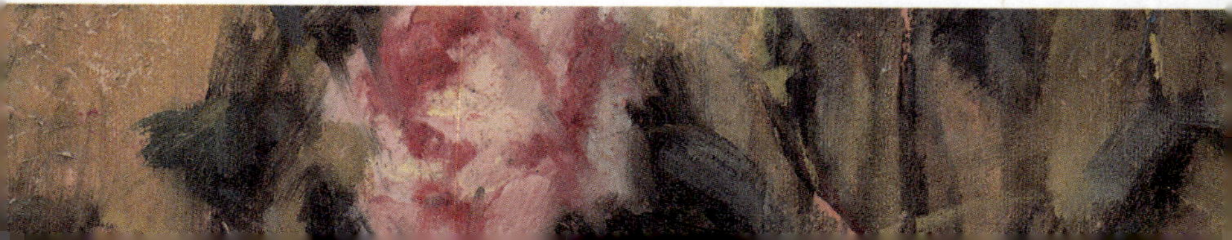

JULY 14

I will both lay me down in peace, and sleep: for thou, Lord, only makest me dwell in safety.

PSALM 4:8

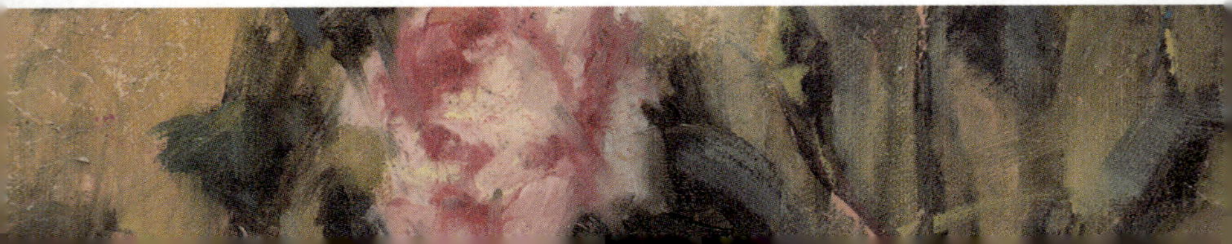

JUNE 20

Not unto us, O Lord, not unto us, but unto thy name give glory, for thy mercy, and for thy truth's sake.

Psalm 115:1

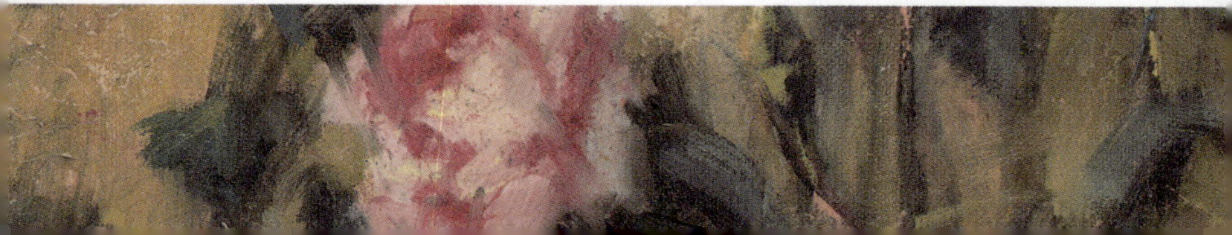

JULY 13

O give thanks unto the Lord; for he is good: for his mercy endureth for ever.

Psalm 118:29

JUNE 21

Though I speak with the tongues of men and of angels, and have not charity, I am become as sounding brass, or a tinkling cymbal.

1 CORINTHIANS 13:1

JULY 12

God is my strength and power:
and he maketh my way perfect.

2 SAMUEL 22:33

JUNE 22

Gracious is the Lord, and righteous;
yea, our God is merciful.

PSALM 116:4-6

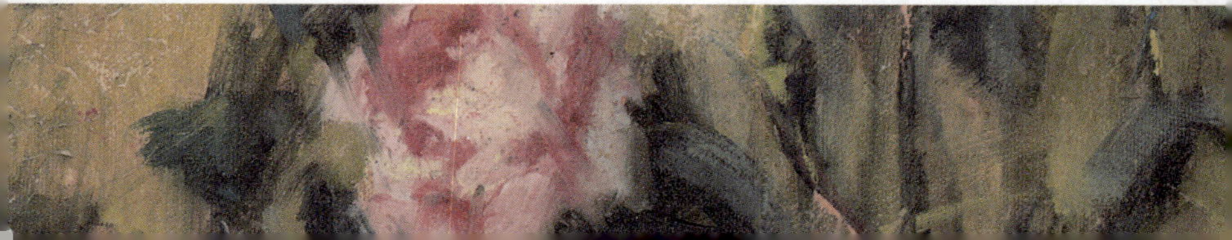

JULY 11

But if from thence thou shalt seek the Lord thy God, thou shalt find him, if thou seek him with all thy heart and with all thy soul.

DEUTERONOMY 4:29

JUNE 23

For the Lord God is a sun and shield: the Lord will give grace and glory: no good thing will he withhold from them that walk uprightly. O Lord of hosts, blessed is the man that trusteth in thee.

PSALM 84:11–12

JULY 10

Not one thing hath failed of all the good things which the Lord your God spake concerning you; all are come to pass unto you, and not one thing hath failed thereof.

JOSHUA 23:14

JUNE 24

Have mercy upon me, O God, according to thy lovingkindness: according unto the multitude of thy tender mercies blot out my transgressions.

PSALM 51:1

JULY 9

For whither thou goest, I will go; and where thou lodgest, I will lodge: thy people shall be my people, and thy God my God.

RUTH 1:16

JUNE 25

Whither shall I go from thy spirit? or whither shall I flee from thy presence? If I ascend up into heaven, thou art there: if I make my bed in hell, behold, thou art there. If I take the wings of the morning, and dwell in the uttermost parts of the sea; Even there shall thy hand lead me, and thy right hand shall hold me.

PSALM 139:7-10

JULY 8

Hear me speedily, O Lord: my spirit faileth: hide not thy face from me, lest I be like unto them that go down into the pit. Cause me to hear thy lovingkindness in the morning; for in thee do I trust: cause me to know the way wherein I should walk; for I lift up my soul unto thee.

PSALM 143:7-8

JUNE 26

Jesus saith unto him, I am the way, the truth, and the life: no man cometh unto the Father, but by me.

John 14:6

JULY 7

It is of the Lord's mercies that we are not consumed, because his compassions fail not. They are new every morning: great is thy faithfulness.

LAMENTATIONS 3:22–23

JUNE 27

Thy mercy, O Lord, is in the heavens; and thy faithfulness reacheth unto the clouds. Thy righteousness is like the great mountains; thy judgments are a great deep.... How excellent is thy lovingkindness, O God! therefore the children of men put their trust under the shadow of thy wings.

PSALM 36:5-7

JULY 6

Be glad in the Lord, and rejoice, ye righteous: and shout for joy, all ye that are upright in heart.

PSALM 32:11

JUNE 28

But as for me, my prayer is unto thee, O Lord, in an acceptable time: O God, in the multitude of thy mercy hear me, in the truth of thy salvation.

PSALM 69:13

JULY 5

I know whom I have believed, and am persuaded that he is able to keep that which I have committed unto him against that day.

2 TIMOTHY 1:12

JUNE 29

But as it is written, Eye hath not seen, nor ear heard, neither have entered into the heart of man, the things which God hath prepared for them that love him.

1 Corinthians 2:9

JULY 4

Let thy mercies come also unto me, O Lord, even thy salvation, according to thy word.

PSALM 119:41

JUNE 30

For ever, O Lord, thy word is settled in heaven. Thy faithfulness is unto all generations: thou hast established the earth, and it abideth. They continue this day according to thine ordinances: for all are thy servants.

PSALM 119:89-91

JULY 3

He shall feed his flock like a shepherd: he shall gather the lambs with his arm, and carry them in his bosom, and shall gently lead those that are with young.

ISAIAH 40:11

JULY 1

For now we see through a glass, darkly;
but then face to face: now I know in part;
but then shall I know even as also I am known.

1 Corinthians 13:12

JULY 2

All the paths of the Lord are mercy and truth unto such as keep his covenant and his testimonies.

PSALM 25:10